SAVE THE Sea Turtles

FIRST EDITION
Series Editor Penny Smith; **Art Editor** Leah Germann; **US Editors** Elizabeth Hester, John Searcy;
DTP Designer Almudena Díaz; **Pre-Production Producer** Nadine King; **Producer** Sara Hu;
Picture Research Myriam Megharbi; **Dinosaur Consultant** Dougal Dixon;
Reading Consultant Linda Gambrell, PhD

THIS EDITION
Editorial Management by Oriel Square
Produced for DK by WonderLab Group LLC
Jennifer Emmett, Erica Green, Kate Hale, *Founders*

Editors Grace Hill Smith, Libby Romero, Michaela Weglinski;
Photography Editors Kelley Miller, Annette Kiesow, Nicole DiMella;
Managing Editor Rachel Houghton; **Designers** Project Design Company;
Researcher Michelle Harris; **Copy Editor** Lori Merritt; **Indexer** Connie Binder; **Proofreader** Larry She
Reading Specialist Dr. Jennifer Albro; **Curriculum Specialist** Elaine Larson

Published in the United States by DK Publishing
1745 Broadway, 20th Floor, New York, NY 10019

Copyright © 2023 Dorling Kindersley Limited
DK, a Division of Penguin Random House LLC
23 24 25 26 10 9 8 7 6 5 4 3 2 1
001-333928-June/2023

All rights reserved.

Without limiting the rights under the copyright reserved above, no part of this publication may be reproduced, stored in
introduced into a retrieval system, or transmitted, in any form, or by any means (electronic, mechanical, photocopying,
recording, or otherwise), without the prior written permission of the copyright owner.
Published in Great Britain by Dorling Kindersley Limited

A catalog record for this book
is available from the Library of Congress.
HC ISBN: 978-0-7440-7269-3
PB ISBN: 978-0-7440-7270-9

DK books are available at special discounts when purchased in bulk for sales promotions, premiums,
fundraising, or educational use. For details, contact: DK Publishing Special Markets,
1745 Broadway, 20th Floor, New York, NY 10019
SpecialSales@dk.com

Printed and bound in China

The publisher would like to thank the following for their kind permission to reproduce their images:
a=above; c=center; b=below; l=left; r=right; t=top; b/g=background

Alamy Stock Photo: Andrey Nekrasov 8c, Doug Perrine 8br, Scubazoo 13cra; **BluePlanetArchive.com:** Doug Perrine 8-9;
Dreamstime.com: Bubbersbb 19bc, Richard Carey 7b (x2), 14br, 21br, Viacheslav Dubrovin 12br,
Benjamin Albiach Galan 22cr, Idreamphotos 1cb, Kjersti Joergensen 16bc, 23tl, Alexey Kornylyev 20-21,
Torsten Kuenzlen 11br, Brian Lasenby 11cra, 23bl, Lemusique 18br, Seadam 23clb, Ekaterina Simonova 18-19,
Stephankerkhofs 6-7, WetLizardPhotography 11c; **Fotolia:** Anna Khomulo 20cb; **Getty Images:** Moment / Ai Angel Gentel
16-17, Moment / M.M. Sweet 5c, Moment / Mark Meredith 13br, 23cl; **Getty Images / iStock:** aimy27feb 4-5, cookelma 6b
Davidevison 12c, Eivaisla 22, kali9 22br, richcarey 14-15, 22bl; **imagequestmarine.com:** Blue Planet Archive /
Doug Perrine 17bc; **naturepl.com:** Doug Perrine 10br, 10-11; **Shutterstock.com:** Rich Carey 4br, SeaSandSun 4c,
Joost van Uffelen 5tr, Seksan Wangjaisuk 3cb, Wirestock Creators 9br

Cover images: *Front:* **Dreamstime.com:** Funkyplayer c, Iuliia Sutiagina b/g;
Back: **Dreamstime.com:** Microvone cla, clb, Natuska cra; *Spine:* **Dreamstime.com:** Funkyplayer

All other images © Dorling Kindersley
For more information see: www.dkimages.com

For the curious
www.dk.com

SAVE THE
Sea Turtles

Ruth A. Musgrave

Seven kinds of sea turtles swim in the sea.

5

hawksbill

This small sea turtle looks for food.

Small. Smaller. Smallest. This smaller sea turtle lives in warm water around the world.

olive ridley

The smallest sea turtle eats crabs.

Kemp's ridley

This sea turtle likes the sandy seafloor

flatback

This big sea turtle
has strong jaws.
It eats sea snails.

loggerhead

Big. Bigger. Biggest.
This bigger sea turtle
eats seagrass.

green

The biggest sea turtle dives deep into the sea.

leatherback

All sea turtles have four long flippers. They use them to swim and dive.

flippers

Sea turtles look for food in the sea. They use their beaks to catch food.

beak

jellyfish

plastic bag

People drop trash on
the ground.
It floats down rivers
and streams.
It ends up in the sea.

That is bad
for sea turtles.

Sea turtles eat trash. They think trash looks like food. They get sick.

jellyfish

You can help sea turtle
Pick up trash no matter
where you live.
You can help, even if
you live far
from the sea.

Glossary

beak
a sea turtle's mouth

flipper
a body part that helps sea turtles swim

leatherback sea turtle
the largest kind of sea turtle

seagrass
a plant that grows in the sea

sea snail
snails that live in the sea

Quiz

Answer the questions to see what you have learned. Check your answers with an adult.

1. What plant do green sea turtles eat?
2. Which sea turtle dives deep?
3. How many flippers do sea turtles have?
4. How does trash end up in the sea?
5. What do sea turtles mistake for food?

1. Seagrass 2. Leatherback sea turtle 3. Four 4. People drop trash, and it floats down rivers and streams 5. Trash